First published in
the United States in 1990 by
Franklin Watts
387 Park Avenue South
New York, NY 10016

Designed and produced by
Aladdin Books and David West
Children's Book Design

© Franklin Watts 1990

Library of Congress Cataloging-in-Publication Data

Nourse, Alan Edward.
    Teen guide to survival / Alan E. Nourse.
        p.   cm.
    Summary: Discusses how teenagers can live defensively and protect
themselves from drug and alcohol use, sexually transmitted diseases, violent
crimes, suicide, and improper eating habits.
    ISBN 0-531-10968-2
    1. Teenagers--United States--Life skills guides--Juvenile literature. 2.
Teenagers--United States--Crimes against--Juvenile literature. 3. Teenagers-
-United States--Substance use--Juvenile literature. 4. Teenagers--United States-
-Sexual behavior--Juvenile literature. 5. Teenagers--Health and hygiene--United
States--Juvenile literature. [1. Life skills. 2. Survival. 3. Conduct of life.] I. Title.
HO796.N68   1990
305.23'5--dc20   90-12267   CIP   AC

Dale-Chall Readability Formula 5.9   Printed in Belgium

The publishers would like to acknowledge that the photographs within this book
have been posed by models or have been obtained from photographic agencies.

This book is not intended as a substitute for the medical advice of doctors. The
reader should consult a doctor in matters relating to his or her health and particularly
in respect to any symptoms that may require diagnosis or medical attention.

CONTENTS

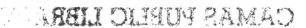

TEEN · GUIDE · TO

SURVIVAL

Alan E. Nourse

Franklin Watts

New York · London · Toronto · Sydney

Chapter One:

Dangerous Times

Many adults remember their teenage years as carefree. But young people have problems and worries just as adults do.

Already you're saying, "That's a weird name for a book! What's 'survival' supposed to mean?"

There was once a clothing store owner who had an ugly green-and-yellow checkered suit for sale. Nobody would buy it. So he promised his clerk an extra $30 if he could sell it to the next person who walked into the store. Half an hour later the clerk came back, covered with blood. His own clothes were torn to ribbons. "Well, I sold that suit," he said.

"But what did the customer do to you?" the owner cried.

"Oh, it wasn't the customer," the salesman said. "It was that seeing-eye dog he had with him."

As that salesman learned, life is full of unexpected dangers. This is especially true for young people growing up today. During your teens most of you are very healthy. But every day, you meet troubles that put your health, or even your life, in danger.

Look at what's happening to four young people very much like yourselves. These stories are true. Just the names have been changed:

Debbie K., age 15, has a problem. This could even be the last day of her life if she doesn't make the right decision.

Debbie and her boyfriend Tom have gone to a beer party at a friend's house. (The parents are away.) Debbie's folks think she and Tom just went to the movies. Now it's very late. Tom has to drive her home because she doesn't have her license yet.

Debbie hasn't had much beer, but Tom has drunk a lot. His voice is slurred. He's unsteady on his feet. Suddenly Debbie knows it would be dangerous and stupid to get in the car with Tom. Two friends have already been killed this year in drunk-driving accidents. But what can she do? It's way past her deadline, and home is five miles away. Should she just take a risk and ride with Tom?

It's a tough choice, but she decides no way. She grits her teeth, takes Tom back to the house, and phones her dad to come get them both. Dad is not going to like this. But at least she and Tom will both be alive next morning.

Dan G., 16 years old, also has a problem, and doesn't know what to do. He and Jerry have been buddies for years. They've shared some beers, smoked some pot, and gotten into trouble together. But lately Jerry's been smoking crack, and wants Dan to try it too. He says it's great, but Dan doesn't like the idea.

Of course, it's tempting. There's some heavy pressure around that you're not really with it if you don't try a little, once in a while. But Dan has heard bad things about crack. He doesn't like what's been happening to Jerry lately, either. Jerry's been different, and making new friends Dan just doesn't trust. Dan has a bad feeling that Jerry's just going to drift away if he doesn't do some crack with him, and that would *really* hurt. What should he do? Who can he talk to? One thing is for sure: he's got to make a choice — a tough and very dangerous choice.

Sixteen-year-old Jennie McK. is scared to death, and doesn't know what to do. Her best friend Tina has been acting very queerly. Tina always used to be cheerful and excited about everything. But lately she's been gray and gloomy, not interested in anything at all. It started when her boyfriend broke up with her because she wouldn't go all the way with him, and it's been getting worse ever since. When she got her acceptance for college next year, she got even gloomier, saying she didn't want to go anyway. Last week Tina started crying for no reason at all. She said she wished she were dead.

That scared Jennie. She knows Tina was thinking about suicide — killing herself — and she sounded like she meant it. Jennie knows teenagers sometimes *do* that. She feels responsible for her friend. But what should she do? Pretend she just didn't hear? Try to talk Tina out of it? Or what? Jennie doesn't even want to think about it, but she can't get it off her mind. She's frightened for Tina, but she doesn't know where to turn.

Fifteen-year-old Kevin B. has a problem, too, even though he pretends it isn't there. Kevin is very popular. He's tall and good looking, and a great athlete. Kevin likes girls and girls like him. He's been having sex with lots of girls for almost two years now. He's not stupid — he knows about "safe sex" and using condoms, and all that. He just doesn't want to bother. Who wants to stop right in the middle of things to put one on? Of course, he has friends who've had bad sexual infections like gonorrhea, and there's one girl everybody knows has genital herpes. But Kevin thinks nothing like that is going to happen to him. The trouble is, Kevin may not get his thinking straight until he finds out the hard way about gonorrhea, or herpes – or even AIDS. And that's too bad, because he doesn't have to take chances with his health, or even his life. It's entirely up to him.

Four young people, and four real problems. There's nothing new about them. Every one of you has run into one or another of them, some time or another. But they're getting more common, and threatening more young people every day. Just look at some facts on the opposite page.

Worried about drinking and driving?
Turn to chapter three (p.17).
Tired of fights and violence at school?
See chapter four (p.27).
Thinking about smoking or drug use?
Go to chapter six (p.45).
Worried about sexual infections?
Check chapter seven (p.53).
Got a friend who's talking about suicide?
See chapter five (p.37).
Wonder what other kids think about these things?
Look at chapter two (p.11).

● There are some 45,000 *deaths* every year in the U.S. from auto accidents. Over half of them involve alcohol in some way. The majority involve teenaged drivers.

● *Suicide* is a major cause of death among young people between the ages of 12 and 20. Everyone feels down at one time or another in their high school years, and the numbers of teen suicides is rising fast.

● *Teen pregnancy* is a real problem in this country. Four out of 10 girls will be pregnant at least once before they're 20. Almost half those teen pregnancies end in abortion. Of course, being pregnant in your teens doesn't usually threaten your life. But it *changes* your life, usually for the worse.

● *Sexually transmitted diseases* are more and more common among teenagers. These infections can make you very sick, ruin your chances of having babies later, or even cause death in some cases.

Lots of teenagers don't want to believe these things. They say it's just other people who have these problems, not them – but they're just sticking their heads in the sand. This book won't tell you how to solve these problems, but it can help you understand what the problems are. Then you can protect yourselves. You can make your own survival decisions. This book will also show you where to get help, when you don't know what to do or what to decide.

Are these just scare stories? Turn the page and find out.

Chapter Two:
What's Really Going On?

Teenagers are faced with a series of tough choices. Decisions made now can affect the rest of your life.

Years ago in a small country in Europe a farm boy walked along the road toward town. A man with a horse cart stopped to give him a ride. As they drove into the village, all the people in the street took off their hats and bowed down. "Why are they doing that?" the boy asked the driver.

"It's the custom. Whenever the King comes to town, everybody takes his hat off and bows down."

"But how do they know the King when they see him?" the boy asked.

"That's easy. The King is the only person who still has his hat on."

Nobody in the street had his hat on. The driver was still wearing his hat. The boy felt his head and found that his hat was still on, too. "Then which of us is King?" he said. "You or me?"

Sometimes it's hard to tell what's really going on. You've all heard reports about bad problems facing teenagers. But how true are they? In 1987, research workers, with the help of the United States Public Health Service, decided to find out. So they went to the best place they could think of for answers — the teenagers themselves.

These researchers took a huge poll of young people in schools all over the United States. It was called the National Adolescent Student Health Survey. It had two goals. First, it hoped to show what problems really *were* threatening teenagers. Second, it wanted to learn what teenagers themselves knew and thought about these problems.

A total of 11,419 eighth- and tenth-grade students were asked to answer some questions. Their classrooms were chosen by lot from 217 different schools in 20 different states. (Of course, the kids didn't give their names.) Some were from big-city schools. Others were from smaller cities, tiny villages, or country areas. Every part of the country was represented.

Nobody *had* to answer any questions. Some parents wouldn't let their children give answers. About 1 out of 10 of the students themselves refused. But those who joined in really felt free to speak out. So their answers were about as close to true as you could ever come.

What were the questions? They covered such topics as *risky driving, fighting and violence in school or out, suicide, the use of tobacco, alcohol, and drugs*, and *sexually transmitted diseases*, including *acquired immune deficiency syndrome (AIDS)*.

What did the students have to say about these things? Their answers were eye-opening.

Risky driving. Half of the students said they had not worn seat belts the last time they rode in a car, truck, or van. Three out of 10 of the eighth-grade students during the past month had ridden in a vehicle driven by someone who had used alcohol or drugs before driving. Four out of 10 tenth-grade students reported the same thing.

Fighting and Violence. Half the boys and 3 out of 10 of the girls reported having been in at least one physical fight during the last year. One-third of all the students said they had been threatened. More than 1 out of 10 had been mugged, and the same number had been physically attacked during the year, at school or on a school bus. Another 1 out of 10 had been attacked outside of school in the same time period.

Among the girls, 1 of every 20 reported that someone had tried to force them to have sex at school during the past year. Two out of 10 said the same thing had happened *outside* of school during the year.

As for deadly weapons, 2 out of 10 boys said they had carried a knife to school at least once during the past year. Many carried knives every day.

Driving demands concentration but alcohol and drugs slow reactions.

One out of every 30 boys had carried a hand gun to school at least once during the year, and *one-third of them said they always carried a gun.*

Suicide. One out of every 4 boys, and 2 out of 5 girls reported they had, at some time during their lives, seriously thought about killing themselves. One out of 10 boys and almost 2 out of 10 girls said they had actually tried to hurt themselves in some way that might have killed them.

Tobacco. About one-third of all students said they had smoked their first cigarette by sixth grade. Half of all eighth-graders and two-thirds of tenth-graders had at least *tried* cigarettes. Almost 1 out of 5 eighth-graders and 1 out of 4 tenth-graders were smoking some cigarettes regularly. Some were already smoking more than one pack a day.

Alcohol and Drugs. Almost one-third of all students reported they had tried alcohol (beer, wine, or hard liquor) before or during sixth grade. By eighth grade 3 out of 4 had used alcohol, and by tenth grade the number was 9 out of 10. One out of 4 eighth-graders and more than 1 out of 3 tenth-graders said they had had five drinks or more on one occasion during the past 2 weeks!

Marijuana wasn't so popular. Only 1 out of 6 of eighth-graders and 1 out of 3 tenth-graders had tried pot, and only 1 out of 20 eighth-graders and 1 out of 7 tenth-graders said they were smoking it once a month or more often. As for cocaine, a far more dangerous drug, 1 of every 20 eighth-graders and almost 1 out of 10 tenth-graders reported having used that drug at least once.

AIDS and other Sexually Transmitted Diseases (STDs). Most students knew how AIDS is passed from person to person. Ninety-four out of 100 knew that having sex with somebody infected with HIV – the "AIDS virus" – would increase their chances of becoming infected with the virus. Ninety-one out of 100 believed that sharing drug needles would also increase their chance of becoming infected. And 86 out of 100 believed that using condoms during sex would decrease their risk of infection. (All these statements are true.)

But many students had some wrong ideas, too. Almost half thought that *donating* blood would increase the risk of HIV infection (not true), and half either thought that "washing after having sex" would protect them from infection(not true), or they weren't sure.

About other sexually transmitted diseases – infections passed from one person to another during sex – students weren't so sure of their facts. Only two-thirds knew that a sore on the sex organs is a common early sign of STDs. Only about half knew that pain when urinating or "going to the bathroom" is another such sign. And only half realized that "waiting to see if the signs go away" was dangerous.

This survey showed clearly that being a teenager today is pretty tough. Knowing how to survive can be very important. What's more, *you* are the ones that face these problems – not your folks, or your teachers, or anybody else. So you need some know-how about survival. You have to make decisions for yourselves about drinking and driving, or fighting and violence in school, or using drugs, or protecting yourselves from sexually transmitted diseases. Nobody else can decide these things for you. Other people can only help. So let's see how plain common sense can help you make sensible "survival" decisions, and where you can go for help if you need it.

Chapter Three:
Drinking, Driving, and Disaster

Driving is great fun but drinking and driving can be a fatal combination, for you and for others.

Teenagers and cars go together like peanut butter and jelly. You get your driver's license just as soon as you possibly can. Whether you have your own car, or use the family's, you love the freedom of wheels. It's proof you're growing up, becoming an adult. You want to get behind the wheel and take off, wherever you please, whenever you please. You think driving is a natural right, like breathing.

Of course, it isn't really a *right*. Driving is actually more of a privilege – a right with strings attached. There are rules you have to follow, or everybody on the road would get wiped out, sooner or later, including you. If you follow the rules, you get to drive. If you don't, the privilege can be taken away. Everybody knows that.

You also know that most kids learn about alcohol early on. Drinking seems like another mark of growing up, becoming an adult. By eighth grade most kids have at least *tried* alcoholic beverages. From then on, quite a few start drinking regularly. Some drink quite a lot. Of course, drinking isn't a right, either. The law says you can't drink legally until you reach a certain age. Everybody knows that, too.

Lots of kids break that law. Whether to drink illegally or not is a decision you have to make for yourself. The penalties for getting caught aren't bad – you usually just get lectured. And lots of kids think that a couple of beers now and then can't possibly hurt anybody.

So we have kids who love to drive, and kids who think a little drinking can't hurt anybody. But what about drinking and *then* driving? That combination is bad for your health – and other people's, too. It *can* hurt. It can even kill you – or others. Drinking plus driving adds up to disaster.

Who says so? What's so bad about driving after just one or two beers? To answer this, let's see what alcohol is all about.

The Influence of Alcohol

Alcohol is a chemical – a colorless liquid. You can't *see* it in a glass of beer, but some of it is in there. Like any other chemical, you can measure it. Whiskey or vodka contain about 4 parts pure alcohol to 6 parts water. Beer contains between 1 and 2 parts pure alcohol to 16 parts water (there's about 7/10 of an ounce of pure alcohol in a 12 ounce beer). Wines contain between 1 and 2 parts alcohol to 10 parts water, depending on the type of wine.

When you drink an alcoholic beverage, the alcohol soaks into your bloodstream within minutes. Once there, it is changed by your liver into other chemicals. In the meantime, it changes how your body works – not your liver, but your kidneys, your heart, and other organs as well.

Most important, it changes how your *brain* works. It slows down your reflexes, your responses, and your thinking. It interferes with muscles that control your eyes, your tongue, and your ability to keep your balance. Even a *little* alcohol has some effect on these things. The more alcohol you have in your bloodstream, the more your brain and muscles are slowed down. It's sort of like dimming the lights, all over.

This is what "feeling" alcohol is all about. Many people find it pleasant, at first. But actually, alcohol starts dimming the lights long before you "feel" anything at all. That's what makes it so tricky – and dangerous. By the time you "feel" it, everything has already slowed way down.

The Brain: Your Personal Computer
What difference does this make?

Say you already know how to drive. Think for a minute about all the split-second decisions you have to make, just driving up to a busy intersection.

Your eyes see the crossing approaching. There are cars ahead of you, cars behind you, cars coming the other way. You have to sense your speed, and calculate how much you have to slow down. You have to calculate the speed of *every other car* approaching the crossing, judge whether they're slowing down or not, and guess where each one of them is going to be – and doing what – by the time you get to the corner.

If you had to work all this out on paper, you'd needs lots of time and complicated math – like calculus – to find all the answers. But your brain is doing it all for you, split second by split second, automatically. Your brain is also checking the street light, judging whether it's going to change or not before you get there. It's also keeping your muscles on alert, so you can step on the brake, step on the gas, turn the wheel, or whatever else turns out to be necessary at whatever split second.

Talk about *decisions!* Your very life can depend on all those decisions being made swiftly and correctly, so you can do exactly the right thing at the right time. Your brain is just a fantastic personal computer, keeping you alive through a simple – but dangerous – thing like driving through an intersection.

Now ask yourself: how much of that split-second computer action do you want to *do without* because a little booze is dimming your lights right then?

What's so bad about driving after a beer or two? You just answered that question. But how much alcohol is "too much?" In one 12-ounce can of beer, you are drinking about 7/10 of an ounce of pure alcohol. That's the same amount there is in an ordinary bar drink of whiskey or vodka. It has already started dimming your lights 10 minutes after you drink it. Two beers equal *two* bar drinks of whiskey or vodka. So if you have six or seven beers in the course of two hours at a party, how smart is it to drive home?

Common sense tells you that there isn't *any* amount of alcohol you can drink and then drive home safely. This isn't some scare story. It's plain fact. So what survival decisions does that fact make you think about? And what can you do to protect yourself from a drinking/driving disaster without looking like an idiot in front of your friends?

Choices

There are several choices you can make.

1) Just don't drink. This can be the best solution of all. It solves a lot of problems. But there are some drawbacks, too.

Why drink in the first place? It's expensive, and illegal when you're

After a crash, police will check for the presence of alcohol.

underage. If you drive at the same time, it can be disastrous. So why do it? You know the answer. It's what everybody does (well, not quite *everybody*, but most.) Teenagers want to be like other teenagers. They don't want to be different or stand out from the others. They want to be part of the crowd, and the crowd drinks.

Why? What does a little alcohol *do*? Well, it's relaxing. It makes you feel good. It makes you feel more cool – which is one of the great things most teens want to feel. You talk more easily, feel more clever, find the jokes funnier. You don't feel so shy. You get along better with the crowd. Of course, if you drink too much, these things get lost. But with just a little, they're *there*.

The trouble is, all of these *feelings* from alcohol are a little bit phony. They come from the alcohol, not you. The fact is, alcohol isn't a stimulant at all – it's a depressant. Even a little of it slows you down. It's also a poison. It eats away, bit by bit, at cells in your brain, your liver, your heart. Finally, it's *addictive*. Regular use turns into a habit that's very hard to get rid of. Not everybody who drinks becomes alcoholic – an addicted drinker – but quite a number do, even young people.

The damage alcohol does isn't noticeable when you only drink a little, now and then. Drink a little more, and the trouble begins. The alcohol irritates your stomach, so you throw up. It gets to your tongue, and your words get slurry. It also gets to your balance and coordination. You tend to lurch around, stumble, get dizzy, fall down. You can hurt yourself badly, even fatally, this way. Movie actor William Holden died of bleeding in his brain after drinking – he slipped and fell, cracking his head against his bedside stand when nobody was around. Actress Natalie Wood drowned while swimming after a bout of drinking.

Finally, drinking spoils your judgment badly *without you realizing* it. That's why drinking and driving is such a deadly combination.

If you decide not to drink, you don't get slowed down. You don't fall. You don't lose your judgment while driving. But others may not like your decision. They may call you a geek if you don't. They may let on there's something wrong with you because of your decision. You're supposed to respect *their* decision to drink, but they won't respect *your* decision not to.

There are ways to get around this. If you decide not to drink on some occasion, or at all, don't make a big fat fuss about it. Do it *quietly*. When somebody offers you a beer, don't say, "No, I never drink." Just say, "I think I'd rather have a Coke right now, thanks." Don't criticize the ones that *do* drink, or act like you're somehow superior. Just hang out and enjoy the party. This approach will help a lot. And in the long run, it will win you the respect of others.

You're the one to decide whether you drink or not. But there's another

Drinking alcohol leads to loss of coordination.

problem to deal with. You may not have drunk a drop, but still have no way to get home without being driven by somebody who has. What do you do about *this*?

It's easy. You plan in advance.

2) The Designated Driver. Some people sneer at this idea. But it's a good answer just the same. When you know there's going to be drinking, make a deal with your friends that one of you who can drive *won't drink* this time, and then stick to it. Then that person drives. You can volunteer, if you've decided not to drink. If everybody wants to drink, draw straws before the party, or sign up on a rotation list. Anybody can live with just Cokes for one evening, if everybody else is depending on him or her. Of course, the designated driver has to stick to his or her promise. No drinking, for that person, means *no drinking*, not even one wine cooler. If somebody makes the deal and then drinks anyway, even a little, don't count on him or her again.

Having a "Designated Driver" will work, if you and your friends make it work. It keeps the problem in *your* hands, where it belongs. And it's a mature, adult way to handle a problem that faces *all* of you.

3) Emergency backup. Most parents don't want their teenage kids to drink. Some just disapprove or discourage it. Some pretend it doesn't happen. Some flatly forbid it – even though it's something they know they can't enforce. But even more, parents really don't want their kids killed or maimed on the road, whether they've broken rules or not.

That means there's room for a deal with your parents to help you stay alive, and relieve *them* of worry, without making a lot of promises you may not keep.

Don't promise them you won't drink if you know you will, or think you may. That's no help. Just promise them that if you ever get in a spot where you can't get home without riding with a drinking driver, you'll call them, and wait for them to come get you. On their side, they promise you they'll come get you, wherever you are, any time of the day or night, *without any hassles*. No questions, no lectures, no punishment, no grounding. That's part of the deal. If they won't promise that, and stick to it, you won't call them the next time. It's as simple as that.

This is not an easy deal to make or keep. But it will do one thing both you and your parents want – help keep you alive. It's a mature, responsible solution to a problem. Since you won't like having to call them, it may encourage you to think twice about your decision about drinking. That's all right. They won't like being called, either, especially the "no hassles" part of it. But like it or not, they'll have more respect for your good judgment and maturity. And that's all right, too.

Some parents just won't go for this, or won't live up to it, and that's too bad. If yours won't, find someone else who will. Talk to your best friend's parent, or a teacher or counselor you like and trust. One warning: be sure your parents, or any others you make the deal with, haven't been drinking all evening before you call. Alcohol slows adults down just as much as it does kids.

4) Better than nothing. There's one other possible choice – not a good one, but better than nothing. If you're the only one around who hasn't been drinking, so there's no other choice, you may just have to drive *without* any license – if you know how to drive. True, that's breaking the law, and you could end up with a ticket. But if it's the *only* choice, it's safer than riding with a drunk driver.

Chapter Four:

Homemade Violence

TV programs are sometimes full of violence and bloodshed. But real-life violence isn't so entertaining.

One problem older people have is that their friends keep dying one by one. An old cowboy was interviewed on his 105th birthday, with his wife, aged 101. The reporter asked how their health was holding up. "Oh, *we're* doing fine," the cowboy said. "But they're shooting all around us."

They're shooting all around you teenagers, too. Violence is part of your everyday world. You hear the news or read the papers. You watch a steady stream of made-up violence on TV or in the movies. You're so used to violence that by now it seems to be "normal." But you tell yourselves it only happens to other people, somewhere else.

Not so. *Homemade* violence is all around you, right in your own schools and streets. It threatens you and your friends every day with danger and sometimes death.

You can't do too much about violence somewhere else. You can do something in your school and on the street, if you know it's happening and want it to stop. At the very least, you can protect yourself from being the next victim.

What's Happening?

We saw what kids themselves knew about violence in the National Student Health Survey back on p. 13. Check that section again. If it makes you think, here are some more things to think about:

1) Among peaceful, civilized people, physical fights are a stupid, dangerous way to solve problems. These fights aren't civilized. The strong ones are just beating up on the weaker ones. That's how animals survive, not people.

2) In a civilized place, nobody should have to worry about being threatened or mugged. When it happens, the person responsible has a serious problem and needs help. There's no place for him or her in a "normal" world.

3) Among civilized people, *nobody* should *ever* be forced to have sex against his or her will. No girl should even have to worry about this. The word for this is rape. It's a crime that destroys people's lives and self-respect. Your body is your own, not somebody else's to just take and use.

4) In a peaceful group, nobody should need to carry deadly weapons for self-protection. When they do, those weapons get used. Just *carrying* the weapons helps violence grow and spread. It's plain common sense that everybody would be far safer if nobody carried any weapons at all.

But what can *you* do about this, you say? You're just one person – *you* can't change anything!

Well, why not? Actually, you can do a lot to protect yourself, and make

*If you carry a knife it's **you** who may end up hurt.*

things better for everybody, if you think about it, and really want to.

The Amazing Power of Pressure

Of course, your school has its own rules about fighting and violence and carrying weapons. Too often, nobody pays much attention to them. Maybe they're not enforced properly. Or everybody may just ignore them because the school is "The Authority" and nobody likes authorities running their lives.

The fact is, students themselves are the ones that make the rules that actually work in most schools, if there *are* any. If you don't make any, then it's everybody for himself or herself, and you live in a jungle.

You know all about *peer pressure*. Your "peers" are your friends and others on an equal footing around you. "Peer pressure" is when others around you put the heat on you to do what *they* think you should do. You may not really want to do some of those things. But you go along with your peers – your friends and others around you – because you want to be part of the crowd. You don't want to stick out too much, or look too different.

It's this peer pressure – what the others think you should do – that makes lots of you start drinking in grade school, even when you don't like the taste of the stuff and don't like the way it makes you feel. You just don't want to be left out. Peer pressure makes some of you start smoking, even though it makes you smell of tobacco, and chokes you, and makes you cough all the time. Smokers look grown-up, the way everybody wants to look. Peer pressure is why so many of you try pot, or crack, or other drugs, even when you know it's stupid and expensive and you're likely to get hooked. You're afraid that your peers will think you look dumb if you don't try it.

That's what "peer pressure" is. Every teenager alive gets pushed around by it. In a way, it "makes the rules" you actually live by in school. They may not be good rules. In fact, they may be very bad for you. But if you don't live by them, you're "out of it." You don't fit in. It takes a lot of guts to walk away from peer pressure and do things differently, *your* way.

But if you think about it, there's no reason you and your friends can't make peer pressure work the other way. You can use it to make *good* rules that protect you against homemade violence. Then the ones who create the violence become the "outsiders" that don't fit in.

Positive Peer Pressure

Take fighting, for example. Fights are a big waste. They don't prove anything, don't accomplish anything, and people get hurt. So suppose both you and your friends decide you just don't want any more fighting around your school.

First, you don't pick fights yourselves. You don't fight at all unless you're forced to. (Of course, that may sometimes happen.) When a fight starts, everybody walks away – no admiring spectators. Everybody soon knows who's picking the fights – they show you who they are. And all of a sudden, because they pick fights, they're the "outsiders." Nobody likes them. Nobody hangs out with them. Nobody approves. If they decide to quit picking fights, they're welcome back, no grudges. Until then, forget it. Very soon, only the really dense ones are still picking fights. There aren't nearly as many fights, any more, and everybody benefits.

Of course, there's something exciting about watching two people duke it out in a hallway or schoolyard free-for-all. It can be hard to just turn your backs and walk away. So why not use peer pressure to keep the fist-fights where they belong – like in a boxing ring – so everybody can watch, if they

The proper place for fist-fights is the boxing ring.

want? Why not involve the coach in refereeing these fights as genuine boxing matches with proper gloves and headgear? It's a lot harder to fight under a clean set of rules in the ring than it is in the school hallway. That way, the ones that just have to fight can fight, but it soon won't be nearly as popular.

Either way, you can do this with positive peer pressure. You say it won't work? Why not? It's a civilized way to make things better for everybody. It can work for a lot of other things, too. It just needs to be set in motion, that's all. And that's not all that hard to do.

1) Buddy up. It's an old idea, and it works. Common sense says you don't go into a dangerous place by yourself. You always go with a buddy or two. Some creep may corner a girl by herself and rape her. But it's a lot harder to do if she's got a couple of friends right there screaming their heads off. Same thing applies if somebody's trying to mug you out in the school parking lot. Buddies mean witnesses, and witnesses mean trouble. Of course, you don't drag your friends along on heavy dates, but you can always double-date. There's safety – and protection – in numbers, especially if there's a lot of bad stuff going on.

2) Identify the problem. It's human nature to pick buddies who think much the same as you do. To get positive peer pressure going, pick one problem at a time. If it's fighting in the schoolyard or on the bus, tackle that. Figure out exactly what you stand for – what you disapprove of and what you don't. Be sure it's important enough to you to take a stand on it. Keep it simple. You aren't trying to reform the world. You just want to cut down on all the dumb fighting going on.

3) Get support from others. Check around for other kids who like this idea, and want to go along with it. We're not talking about taking vows or anything, just general support. Lots of kids will say, "I'm all for it, if it'll work." That's all you need. It doesn't take a million people to start a trend –

just a few. Then, if it makes sense, others will join in.

4) Act – don't talk. This may be most important of all. Don't talk a lot about what you're going to do. Just quietly do it. Start walking away when a fight starts. Start turning your backs on the fight-pickers. Don't try to tell them how they should behave, just walk away from them. *Show* your disapproval, don't talk it. They'll get the message soon enough. Be consistent – don't disapprove of one but approve of another. That just tells people you're not serious.

5) Get school backing – if you think it will help. Once you've got something going and working, get help from your school authorities, if you think it will do any good. (Maybe it won't.) Maybe they can enforce their own rules better. You don't need to make a formal announcement to the principal. Just pick a teacher or counselor that a lot of the kids know and

Teachers will help if you confide in them.

33

trust, and quietly pass the word. Say that the kids are trying to get the fights stopped, so please back them up. The school authorities will know about it in no time. You might be surprised how happy they'll be to have a little student action going on.

The same positive peer pressure can work against other kinds of homemade violence, too. Who *needs* to carry knives or guns to school? If they think they do, they don't fit in. Maybe you can't completely stop this with peer pressure alone. But you can reduce it, and reduce the need for it, at the same time. A lot of weapons-carrying is really nothing but a big tough guy display, anyway – which caveman has the biggest club? If nobody admires these cavemen any more, it's much less fun to carry weapons, and everybody's safer.

The same thing goes for shakedowns and muggings. The ones who do it suddenly find that they're the outsiders. What's more, it becomes easier to report these events. Nobody's ratting on anybody who doesn't deserve it. The same thing for sexual harassment. Of course, every guy or girl makes his or her own reputation here. Once you have a reputation, you're stuck with it unless you decide to change it. That's entirely up to you.

Not everybody will like positive peer pressure. It keeps some people from acting like animals any time they feel like it. But it works, if enough kids want to make decent rules and then live by them.

Other Approaches

Other things will help, too. There's an old saying, "The Devil finds work for idle hands." If there's nothing more exciting going on than picking fights, people will pick fights, just because they're bored. The same with hassling girls or smoking crack. Lots of kids think school is deadly. But there's no reason you can't put some life into it, with a little imagination.

Recently some kids in a New Jersey school got interested in Medic One lifesaving. They got together with a good biology teacher. They contacted the local fire department that ran the Medic One emergency car. First they learned CPR. That's "cardio-pulmonary resuscitation" – the things you can do to start a person's heart beating again when it's stopped, or to get him breathing again. Then the kids learned on-the-scene first aid. With that knowledge, they started going out on Medic One calls – saving lives.

Some of their classmates thought they were idiots, but *they* didn't. They weren't picking fights or hassling girls. They didn't have time. They were too busy doing something exciting, and interesting, and useful. And they had to keep their grades up to stay in the program.

It doesn't have to be that difficult. It can be such things as field trips, or electronics repairs, or rockhounding, or neighborhood urban renewal projects. Many schools have the start of such programs, with interested teachers, good counselors, and meeting facilities. You kids yourselves can expand such programs. Or you can start your own, if there aren't any. Just talking with interested teachers or counselors can turn up ideas. And thinking up new ideas just naturally leads to more new ideas.

Homemade violence is far worse in some places than others. But it's getting steadily worse *everywhere*. Nobody from the outside is going to stop it. But you and your friends hold the key, because you *can* do something.

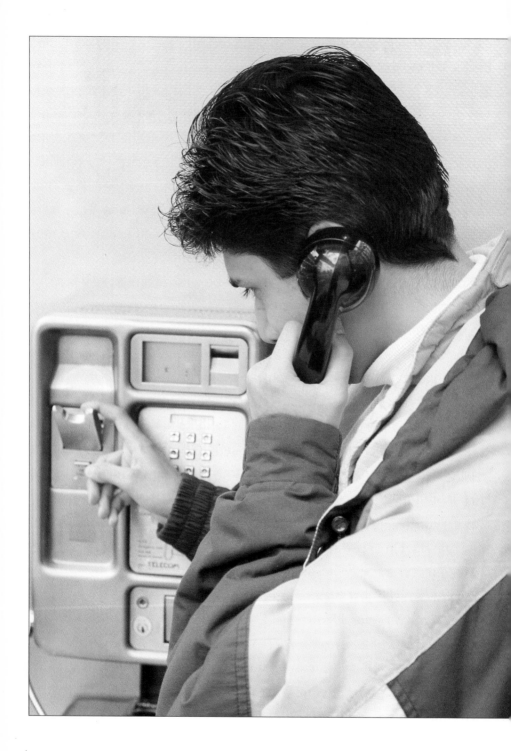

Chapter Five:

Depression and Suicide

If problems seem too much to cope with alone, it's good to talk things through with someone who understands.

Suicide – people killing themselves – is scary. You hear about it all the time. It's a terrible thing. It doesn't make sense. Nobody understands it. And it doesn't just happen somewhere else, either. Chances are you've already seen it in your own school. Second to car accidents, suicide is the *most common* cause of death among teenagers.

Suicide doesn't just happen. People think about it first. The National Student Health Survey showed that 1 out of every 4 boys and 2 out of every 5 girls said that they had seriously thought of killing themselves at some time in their lives. One out of 10 boys and almost 2 out of 10 girls said they had actually tried to injure themselves in some way that might have killed them.

So suicide is a common thing for kids to think about. But there's something else just as common among teenagers, if not more so, and that's depression. Suicide and depression are very closely related.

What's Depression?

"Depression" is a fancy doctor's word for feeling gray and gloomy and useless and just not interested in anything.

Everybody gets a little down once in a while. Call it the blues or the gloomies or the Monday morning blahs, or whatever. It comes and goes, usually pretty quickly. This is a normal part of the way your brain works. It can make your day look absolutely dismal. But after a few hours, or a day or so, it all clears up and everything's fine again. That's normal, too. It's your brain's natural sense of self-preservation kicking in.

That kind of mild, now-and-then blahs isn't what we mean by depression. It isn't abnormal or dangerous. But when the blues come and stay – and stay – and stay – and you can't shake them off for days or weeks, that's something else. *That* is depression. It is abnormal, and dangerous. It makes people start thinking about suicide.

Two Kinds Of Depression

There are two kinds of depression that can come, and hang on, and won't go away.

Sometimes people get badly depressed because depressing things are happening to them. A girl gets pregnant when she doesn't want to be, and doesn't know what to do about it. She gets depressed. A guy gets hooked on crack, and doesn't have money to buy it, and things are starting to unravel, and *he* gets depressed. A kid has a running battle with his parents about everything, and it gets worse, not better, and they hate him and he hates them, or so it seems, and he gets depressed. Or a girl breaks up with her boyfriend, and the bottom drops out of her life. Of *course* she's depressed.

This kind of depression happens when things outside start pressing in. Bad things happen, and you react by getting depressed. That's why it's called *reactive* depression. It's not good – long-lasting depression *never* is – but at least it's understandable. And if you can fix up the outside problem, the depression may clear up before it gets dangerous. If it doesn't , it becomes very dangerous indeed, because it makes you feel lousy and can easily start you thinking about ways to make it stop – including suicide.

The other kind of depression is more tricky. It turns up for no apparent reason whatever. It's just there. It *isn't* understandable. It pops up from inside you, without any help from the outside. Doctors think it's caused by changes in the chemical activity in the brain. Sometimes it turns up suddenly. More often, it sneaks up on you slowly and quietly. You don't even know it's there for weeks or even months. Everything just slows down. You lose interest in school, friends, everything. You don't feel like doing *anything*. You just sit there. You get gloomier and gloomier, and you can't shake it off.

Either kind of depression can do weird things to your head. You start thinking things that don't make sense – things you wouldn't dream of thinking ordinarily. Things like: *What's the use? There's no way out. Why hang around? Why not just put an end to it?*

The trouble is, you don't understand that this thinking is weird. It seems "normal" and "reasonable" to you. Your friends may think it's weird, but not you. They don't see how you can really think such things. They may just not believe you. They may think you're joking, or making a big deal out of nothing.

Some other things can make either kind of depression a lot worse.

Emotional upsets – fights with your folks, for example, or breaking up with a steady – can make it worse. Drinking can make it worse, because alcohol is a *depressant* drug all by itself. Using pot or crack can make it worse, too. With them, your head is already mixed up, *without* any depression. Pile depression on top, and you've got real trouble.

What Can You Do?

By the time you start thinking about suicide – or a friend of yours does – it's already five minutes to midnight. You'd better do something fast, or it could be too late.

In either case, the first thing to do is admit that you can't handle it alone. You're in water over your head. You need help.

Years ago there wasn't much to be done about depression except wait

Counselors and teachers can help work through a crisis.

for it to go away. That's not true any more. Today most depression can be cleared up very quickly. Sometimes just talking to an expert counselor is all you need to get on the right road. Your school authorities can help you connect with that kind of help. In other cases, simple antidepressant medicines (depression-fighting medicines) can do wonders. Any doctor in practice knows these medicines and how to use them. Getting expert counsel or using the right medicines can be like grabbing a life-preserver when you're drowning. It can save your life.

When you realize that you're depressed, or even think you are, the first thing to do is to tell somebody. Don't try to deal with it alone. Tell your parents. Tell your best friend. Tell a counselor or teacher you trust at school. Tell somebody.

Second, see a doctor and tell him or her what's going on. Don't worry about not having insurance, or paying for it, or anything else. It's not going to cost that much. You don't have to see a psychiatrist – any doctor will do. If the doctor you see doesn't take it seriously, or tries to talk you out of it, or doesn't believe you, find another one who does. If medicine is ordered, buy it and take it exactly as directed. Don't fool around. Postpone any other decisions, for the time being. It may take a week or more for any medicine to start working. Then, *follow up* with the doctor, to make sure the depression is clearing up and staying cleared up.

When you have a friend who's depressed, listen to him or her and believe what you hear, especially if there's even a hint about suicide. Never mind if what your friend says seems weird and unreal – take it very seriously. Don't joke about it. Don't shrug it off or try to talk the person out of it – it won't work. Urge your friend to get help, to tell somebody else or see a doctor. If he or she won't, then *you* get help without wasting time. Don't try to handle it alone – it's over your head. Sound the alarm to *somebody*. As a friend, you're not "betraying a trust" when you do this.

You may just be saving a life.

Most teachers or counselors or other school authorities have had training and experience dealing with this sort of crisis. At least they will know what help exists in your community for dealing with it. But there's other help you can seek out directly. Your parents – or your friend's parents – may be startled by the idea that serious depression is going on. Depressed kids often don't talk to anybody or pass out any hints that something is out of line. But parents aren't stupid. They have the means to get help from doctors or counselors if they know something is wrong. In addition, almost every community today has some kind of Crisis Hotline operating. This is a telephone manned by people who are trained to help people in trouble hang on until help can be found. You'll find a number listed in any phone book under **Crisis Line** or **Crisis Clinic**. Finally, any minister, school nurse, or Public Health Department official can be a source of help.

Not all suicidal thoughts occur because of depression. But the two are so often connected that you simply have to be alert. There are different possible ways to deal with these thoughts. The worst possible way is to *act* on them, or allow a friend to act on them, by just not seeing or doing anything. There's no *need* for kids to think about injuring or killing themselves. The causes for that thinking can be cleared up if they're spotted in time.

A problem shared is a problem halved.

Chapter Six:

Tobacco Road and Drug Row

Friends may say it's cool to smoke, but once you've tried cigarettes or drugs it may not be so easy to stop.

Suicide is not the only form of self-destruction that kids can get stuck in. Other ways are just slower.

In Erskine Caldwell's novel *Tobacco Road*, a man bought a brand new car, and completely destroyed it in three days. Every time he ran the car into a stump, turned it over in a gulley, or bashed in a headlight, he said, "Well, it didn't hurt the runnin' of it none." It didn't – for about three days. By then, the car was a useless heap of junk.

Teenagers' use of tobacco or drugs has a lot in common with what happened to that new car. It doesn't hurt the runnin' of them none – until the axe drops sometime later.

The National Student Health Survey told us about teenage tobacco and drug use. Six out of 10 students had at least tried cigarettes by tenth grade. Almost 1 out of 5 eighth-graders, and 1 out of 4 tenth-graders, were smoking regularly. Some were smoking more than a pack a day.

Marijuana isn't as popular as it once was. Lots of kids said they'd tried it, but only 1 in 20 eighth-graders and 1 in 7 tenth-graders said they used it once a month or more. As for cocaine, overall, 1 in 20 eighth-graders and 1 in 10 tenth-graders reported having used it. Cocaine and crack are much more prevalent in some schools than others. And some teenagers are already shooting up heroin. What does all this mean?

Children are quick to imitate the habit of smoking.

Tobacco Road

Cigareets is the bane of the whole human race.
You look like a monkey with one in your face.
Now hear me, dear friend, now hear me dear brother:
A fire on the one end, a fool on the tother.*

What's there to say about smoking that you don't already know? Not much. Most smokers can't tell you *why* they smoke, except that they "like it." Tobacco smoke is filled with tars and gases that beat up your air tubes and lungs, a little at a time. Anyone who smokes regularly has *acute bronchitis* – inflamed, irritated air tubes .

The really bad stuff in tobacco is *nicotine*. It's a violent poison. A tiny drop is enough to kill a rabbit. In dribs and drabs, from smoking (or chewing tobacco or taking snuff) it's a powerful stimulant. It makes your heart work harder, and other things in your body work faster. After a while, the tars and nicotine in tobacco cause heart disease and lung cancer, as well as other cancers. But it's hard for teenage smokers to get seriously worried about bad things that may happen 20 or 30 years later.

What you can and should consider is that nicotine is extremely *addictive*. It doesn't take long to get thoroughly hooked. Once you're hooked, you may stay hooked for the rest of your life. Nicotine addiction is one of the hardest to break. Many people *do* it, but only after a long, hard fight. Lots of people find they just can't.

Of course, the cigarette makers never mention *addiction* in any of their ads urging young people to smoke. Addiction is why they're so eager to get you smoking early. They *know* most teenage smokers will be lifelong

* From the country song *Cigareets and Whuskey and Wild, Wild Women*, by Red Ingle.

47

customers. Those companies don't care about you, or the long-term consequences of smoking. All they want is your money, *now*.

Think about this when you make your decision about smoking. The message about protecting your body and staying alive on Tobacco Road is very simple. **If you don't smoke or use tobacco yet, don't start for any reason. If you already smoke (or chew tobacco or take snuff), stop just as fast as you can, and don't start again**. It's *much* easier to stop when you've just started than five or ten years later.

Marijuana Dreams

There's probably not much you don't already know about marijuana, either. It may not be quite all it's cracked up to be, because less is being used by kids now than, say, ten years ago. But some of you still use it.

Teenagers go for pot because they think (l) it makes them feel good, (2) it's inexpensive, (3) it's harmless, and (4) it's fun to do with their friends. Actually, none of these things are quite true.

● While pot makes some of you "feel good," it makes others sick to their stomachs. Some just don't like what it does to their heads. Sad to say, many of you feel a lot of peer pressure to use the stuff even when you'd really rather not.

Marijuana or *cannabis* contains a drug called tetrahydrocannabinol or just *cannabinol* that acts on your brain. It makes you feel relaxed and sociable. It changes your sense of time passing. It seems to make pop music more interesting and enjoyable. (That's why pot is so popular at rock concerts.) It often seems to make foods taste better. For some people, it seems to make having sex more fun. But all of these things are basically phony. They're just the action of a drug. They're not *you*.

● Inexpensive? Not really. Pot is cheaper than crack or heroin, maybe even cheaper than alcohol. But nobody hands it out free for very long. If somebody shares a stash with you, you're expected to share in return, sometime later. And it does cost money.

● It's not quite "harmless," either. Pot smoke is all full of gases that beat up your air tubes and give you bronchitis. The drug effects last for hours, so a joint before school in the morning is going to muddle your head in school all day long. Cannabinol piles up in your body's fat, and stays there for weeks. (It can be detected in your urine for more than a month.) It's not physically addictive, like nicotine or crack, but you tune in to it *mentally*, so it's hard to quit.

The worst thing is that a pot smoker may just zone off on school and classes and other activities. Your brain doesn't work well for you, even when you want it to. And marijuana and driving are murder. It's very easy to go roaring down the highway at 95, feeling like you're just floating along

Taking illegal drugs is highly dangerous.

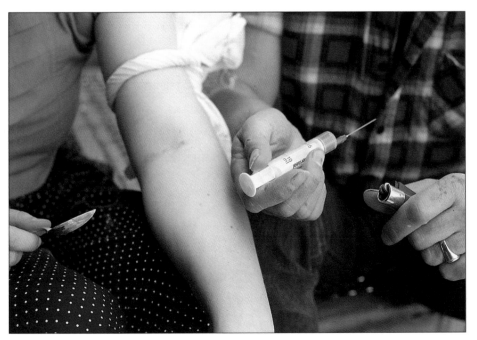

at 35. That is *really* life-threatening.

● Pot may be fun to do with your friends, but there are lots of other things that don't carry the price and danger. Whether to use pot at all or not is *your* decision. Nobody is going to make it for you (your parents or others may *try*, but they don't control you.) If you're already using it, it isn't as hard to stop as with tobacco or alcohol. Think about it. If you really respect your body and mind – the best things you have going for you – common sense will tell you that you shouldn't deliberately poison them with something like this.

Drug Row

Crack, cocaine, heroin, crystal, PCP (angel dust), acid, & company – most of you already know these are a bad scene from the ground up. Bad for you, and bad for staying alive. There's no room here to talk about all the physical, mental, and addiction effects of these things. There are good books you can read for all the facts you need to make your own decisions about using them or not. See Additional Reading on p. 59.

As far as staying alive is concerned, dealing and using these drugs can quickly turn your school or community into an unlivable jungle. Gangs take over. Drug deals go sour and people get killed. Completely uninvolved people get hurt or killed in random drive-by shoot-ups. Drug dealers don't care. They want your money, and they want you hooked so you have to buy more. That's all they want. Then you have to deal or steal to get the money. The dealers couldn't care less what happens to you or anybody else. Nice people. They already include some of your classmates. You'd better believe it.

There's one even worse side. Drugs get shot up, and dirty needles get passed around. All of a sudden you've got friends who are infected by HIV (the AIDS virus) whether they know it or not. They're all set to pass the virus on to anybody who shares needles with them or has sex with them.

Once all this gets started in your school or community, you've got a terrible problem getting rid of it. There's really only one way that you, yourself, can protect yourself from this problem: don't join it. Decide that there's no way you're going to get involved. Turn your back on peer pressure. If *anybody* – even your own "best friend" – is trying to turn you on to this, you already know your enemy. You know who to walk away from and never look back. Living defensively is the only answer here. *You* have to decide.

Chapter Seven:
The Minefields Of Sex

Decisions about sex are some of the most important in your life. Possible consequences need to be thought about very carefully.

We know from the survey that some teenagers are having sex, or thinking about it seriously, as early as fourth or fifth grade. More and more of them make this decision as they grow older and more mature. Of course, many don't have sex, and don't want to yet.

Many of those who *do* have just one partner. The word for this is *monogamous*. It simply means "one sexual partner only." But some have sex with several, or even many, partners. The word for this is *promiscuous* – an unpleasant word which simply means "several different sex partners from time to time." Whether they do have sex or not almost all teenagers are *interested* in sex. This interest is absolutely normal as kids grow up.

For most young people, sexual experiences are very pleasant. But for those who do have sex, there are also some *un*pleasant things to think about. It's a little like walking through a minefield in a battle zone. You have to watch your step.

For example, there's the plain fact that some people around you may disapprove – especially your parents, or even some of your peers. There's the risk of getting pregnant when you don't want to, unless you always

Condoms help prevent the spread of sexually transmitted diseases.

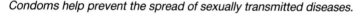

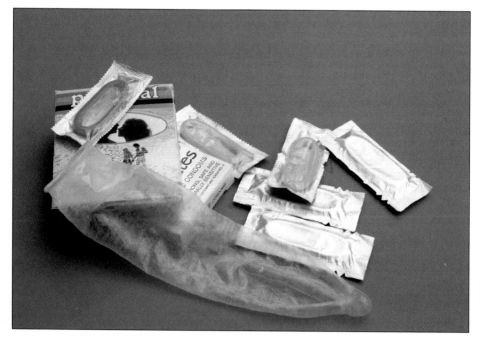

take *very careful* precautions to prevent this. There's the risk of being hurt emotionally. This can happen if you start having sex before you're mature enough to deal with the tough personal problems that arise from sex relationships.

There's also the risk of contracting *sexually transmitted diseases* or STDs. These are infections that are passed on from person to person during sex. They can damage your health, or prevent you from having babies later on. These infections include AIDS – a thoroughly deadly infection. The virus that causes it will, in most cases, kill you, and you must take measures to keep from getting infected in the first place.

You'll find books in your school or public libraries with all kinds of facts about sexually transmitted diseases, safe sex, and birth control. I've written some myself. (See *Teen Guide to Safe Sex, Teen Guide to Birth Control*, and *AIDS (Revised Edition)*, all published by Franklin Watts. We only have room here to list some of the basic "rules of living defensively" that you need to know just to stay alive and basically unharmed as a result of having sex.

Sexually transmitted diseases (STDs). These infections include *gonorrhea, syphilis, genital herpes, chlamydia infection*, and a number of others. *All* are passed from one person to another by having sex with an infected person. Either sex can transmit these diseases, and either sex can be infected.

Not having sex with anybody at all is the best possible protection against these infections. If you don't have sex, you won't get STDs. If you do have sex, you can reduce the risk of catching these diseases in two simple ways:
● Be sure the boy always puts on a latex rubber condom before any

sexual contact begins.

● Be sure the girl always uses a sperm-killing gel or cream containing the chemical *nonoxynol-9* in her vagina before sex begins.

A latex rubber condom will keep STD germs, including viruses, from passing through from person to person. The nonoxynol-9 kills sperm cells on contact. It also helps kill STD germs as well. Note: these self-protective steps are not absolutely fail-safe. You can still get infected in spite of them, especially if you don't use the condom or spermicide properly. But the chances of infection are far less if you take these steps. (For more details about using condoms and spermicides properly, see *Teen Guide to Safe Sex.*)

Unwanted pregnancies. Again, the best possible protection is not to have sex with anybody at all until you are fully prepared to handle a pregnancy and *want* to be pregnant. If you do have sex, the combination of condom-and-spermicide mentioned above will also help prevent an unwanted pregnancy. This precaution doesn't always work here, either. There are much better, more reliable methods of birth control. But the condom-and-spermicide combination works better than no precautions at all. (For more details about different methods to prevent unwanted pregnancies, see *Teen Guide to Birth Control.*)

AIDS. This particular sexually transmitted disease is dangerously different from any other. AIDS means "**A**cquired **I**mmune **D**eficiency **S**yndrome." The disease can result from infection with HIV (the "AIDS virus"). This virus is spread from one person to another in two main ways:

● By sharing dirty drug needles with someone who is already infected

Relationships don't have to be sexual to be fun!

with the AIDS virus; or

● By having sex with someone who is already infected with the AIDS virus.

There's no way that you can tell, *for certain*, that the person you have sex with, or share a dirty needle with, isn't infected. That person may not even know it himself or herself. If they *do* know it, they may lie to you about it. What you need to understand is that once you are infected, there is no way to get rid of the virus. And if the virus causes you to get AIDS, the disease can be fatal.

How do you protect yourself from this kind of danger? First, *don't share needles with anyone*, anywhere or any time, for any reason whatsoever, period.

Second, don't have *unprotected* sex with anyone, anywhere, any time, unless you are very certain that person has never shot up injectable drugs, and does not have an HIV infection. (The only way a person can tell that is by having a recent test for AIDS antibodies. These are chemicals that appear in the blood after a person is infected. But even *that* isn't foolproof. It may take weeks or even *years* after a person is infected before the antibodies show up on a test.)

Once again, the best possible protection against catching HIV infection is not to have sex with anyone unless you've known that person very well for a long time, and then only with one person at a time. The more sex partners you have, the greater the chances that one of them is infected and can give you the virus. If you do have sex, practice *safe* sex by using the combination of condom-and-spermicide we talked about above. Do it *always*, every time you have sex, without fail. This is just common-sense defensive living, nothing more. (For more detail about safe sex, living defensively, and AIDS, see *AIDS (Revised Edition)* by Alan E. Nourse, M.D.)

Survival is no joke for teenagers these days. To stay alive and healthy, you first have to know the dangers, and then have some idea how to protect yourselves. That's why this book is written. It doesn't have all the answers. But *you* have the power to make decisions – good ones or not – that can make a big difference. This book has suggestions for survival. Now it's up to you.

Additional Reading

Berger, Gilda. *Addiction: Its Causes, problems, and Treatment*. New York: Franklin Watts, 1982.

_____ . Violence and Drugs. New York: Franklin Watts, 1989.

Black, Beryl. *Coping with Sexual Harassment*. New York: Rosen Group, 1987.

Bode, Janet. *The Voices of Rape*. New York: Franklin Watts, 1990.

Cohen, Daniel and Cohen, Susan. *A Six-Pack and a Fake I.D.* New York: M. Evans, 1988.

Crook, Marion. *Teenagers Talk About Suicide*. Ontario: University of Toronto Press, 1988.

Hyde, Margaret and Forsyth, Elizabeth. *Suicide: The Hidden Epidemic*. New York: Franklin Watts, 1986.

Leder, Jane M. *Dead Serious: A Book For Teenagers About Teenage Suicide*.

New York: Antheneum, 1987.

McFarland, Rhoda. *Coping With Substance Abuse*. New York: Rosen Group, 1989.

Nourse, Alan E., M.D. *AIDS, Revised Edition*. New York: Franklin Watts, 1988.

_____ . *Herpes*. New York: Franklin Watts, 1985.

Phelps, Janice Keller, M.D., and Nourse, Alan E., M.D. *The Hidden Addiction and How To Get Free*. Boston: Little, Brown, 1986.

Silverstein, Herma. *Teenage Depression*. New York: Franklin Watts, 1990.

Taylor, L.B., Jr. *Driving High: The Hazards of Driving, Drinking and Drugs*. New York: Franklin Watts, 1983.

Woods, Geraldine and Harold. *Cocaine*. New York: Franklin Watts, 1985.

Glossary

Acute bronchitis – active irritation of the lining of the bronchial tubes (air tubes) in the lungs. May be caused by infection, or by inhaling tobacco smoke or marijuana smoke.

Addictive – any drug or other substance that causes the user to have a physical or mental craving for more. Drugs such as nicotine, cocaine, or alcohol are strongly addictive.

AIDS – **A**cquired **I**mmuno-**D**eficiency **S**yndrome. A fatal disease caused by infection by the Human Immunodeficiency Virus (HIV) which leads to a slow destruction of the body's immune system. Since HIV can be passed from one person to another by having sex, AIDS is a *sexually transmitted disease* or STD.

Alcholic – a person who has become addicted to alcohol. About 1 out of every 10 people who drink alcohol becomes an alcoholic.

Anti-depressant drugs – medicines that help fight off depression and make it disappear.

Cannabis or **Cannabis sativa** – the correct botanical name for the marijuana plant.

Chlamydia infection – a sexually transmitted disease or STD caused by a viruslike germ called *Chlamydia trachomatis*. Affects the urinary tract in males and females, and the vagina, cervix, and tubes of females. When untreated, an important cause for sterility (inability to have babies) in females.

Depressant – any drug or substance that depresses or slows down the normal action of the brain, heart, or other organs. Alcohol is a common depressant drug.

Depression – a feeling of "blues" or gloominess that comes and stays for long periods of time. *See also* **Reactive depression**.

Designated driver – a person who agrees not to drink at a party or gathering so that he or she can safely drive others home.

Genital herpes – a sexually transmitted disease or STD caused by a herpes virus. Causes recurring, painful, infectious sores on the sex organs.

Gonorrhea – a very contagious sexually transmitted disease or STD caused by the gonorrhea germ *Neisseria gonorrhea*. Infects the urinary tract in males and females, and the vagina and tubes of the female. A major cause of sterility (inability to have babies) in females.

HIV – **H**uman **I**mmunodeficiency **V**irus. A virus that infects human beings and can cause AIDS in many cases. *See also* **AIDS**.

Monogamous – a person who has sex with only one partner.

Nicotine – a strongly addictive drug present in all forms of tobacco – cigarettes, chewing tobacco, snuff, etc.

Peer – a friend or classmate on an equal footing with you.

Peer pressure – group pressure. A strong feeling that you must behave the way your peers think you should behave, or do what they think you should do, however undesirable, for the sake of appearances.

Positive peer pressure – purposely using peer pressure to establish *desirable* or "survival" rules of behavior, such as no fighting at school, no weapons carried to school, etc.

Promiscuous – a person who has sex

Call for help

ith many partners.

eactive depression – depression that ∶curs as a *reaction* because depressing ⊿tside things are happening to a person.

exual harassment – unwelcome or ¬desired sexual annoyances or advances from others. Can be as simple as ⊔ughing at or bad-mouthing someone of ╷e opposite sex, on the one hand, or as ∍rious as trying to force another person ⊙ have sex against his or her will, on the ⋅her hand.

yphilis – a dangerous sexually transmit- ∙d disease or STD caused by the spiral- ╷aped bacillus *Treponema pallidum*. If ┐discovered and untreated, this disease ∍n cause widespread destruction of the ╷ajor blood vessels, heart, brain, or other ⋅gans. The infection can eventually be ∙tal.

TDs – **S**exually **T**ransmitted **D**iseases. ∩y diseases or infections spread from ∩e person to another during sex.

etrahydrocannabinol – the active drug ∙ the marijuana plant.

The following is a list of toll-free hotlines, especially set up by government agencies and private organizations to help you.

National AIDS Hotline: 1-800-342-AIDS Provides confidential information, referrals, and educational material on AIDS.

National Youth Crisis Hotline: 1-800-448-4663 Will talk with you and make referrals for all types of crises: pregnancy, running away, suicide, AIDS, drugs, physical abuse, family problems. Provides runaways with various church and shelter information and counseling referrals.

Suicide 24-Hour Hotline: 1-800-333-4444 Humanistic Mental Health Foundation provides a national suicide, drug, alcohol, and cocaine addiction hotline, plus crisis intervention of all kinds.

National Institute on Drug Abuse Hotline: 1-800-662-HELP Provides information and makes referrals. Calls 9 a.m. – 3 p.m. EST, Monday – Friday; 12 p.m. – 3 p.m., Saturday, Sunday.

Alcohol Hotline: 1-800-ALCALLS Provides information, literature, guidance, crisis intervention. English/Spanish. Confidential.

National Crisis Hotline: 1-800-367-2727 ASAP Treatment Center. Will talk with you, answer questions and provide referrals for drug, alcohol, suicide, and depression.

National Runaway Hotline: 1-800-621-4000 Offers help and referrals to runaway shelters and counseling services throughout the United States.

Index

Photographic credits
Cover: Roger Vlitos; pages 4, 13, 16, 26, 29, 33, 36, 40, 42, 44, 46, 49, 51, 52 and 54: Marie-Helene Bradley; page 10: The *Daily Telegraph* Newspaper; pages 21 and 31: J. Allan Cash Library; page 23: Vanessa Bailey.